I0815977

A FOUR-LEGGED SOLDIER IN THE SECOND WORLD WAR

WHITEY'S JOURNEY

WRITTEN BY
KELSEY LONIE

ILLUSTRATED BY
RENEE HANSEN

Heritage House Publishing Company Ltd.
heritagehouse.ca

Cataloguing information available from Library and Archives Canada
978-1-77203-557-5 (hardcover)
978-1-77203-559-9 (e-book)

Cover and interior book design by Setareh Ashrafologalai

Photographs on pages 42–43 courtesy of Library and Archives Canada, e011848115 (left) and e011848116 (right).

The interior of this book was produced on FSC®-certified, acid-free paper, processed chlorine free, and printed with vegetable-based inks.

Heritage House gratefully acknowledges that the land on which we live and work is within the traditional territories of the Lkwungen (Esquimalt and Songhees), Malahat, Pacheedaht, Scia'new, T'Sou-ke, and W̱SÁNEĆ (Pauquachin, Tsartlip, Tsawout, Tseycum) Peoples.

We acknowledge the financial support of the Government of Canada through the Canada Book Fund (CBF) and the Canada Council for the Arts, and the Province of British Columbia through the British Columbia Arts Council and the Book Publishing Tax Credit.

29 28 27 26 25 1 2 3 4 5

Printed in China

To my parents, who sat with me for hours when I was a child, reading books. They sparked my imagination, my love of a good story, and my desire to communicate through words.

K.L.

For Mom and Dad. Thank you for cheering me on from the very beginning.

R.H.

ACKNOWLEDGEMENTS

Many thanks to the editorial team at Heritage House for believing in this special story and turning my vision into a reality.

Special thanks to Gord Crossley, curator at the Fort Garry Horse Museum and Archives in Winnipeg, Manitoba. He introduced me to Whitey in 2023 and sent me a wealth of material to work with. His generosity made crafting Whitey's story possible. And to Michael MacDonald from Library and Archives Canada for sourcing even more photographs of Whitey.

I am eternally grateful to my amazing illustrator, Renee Hansen, who brought *Whitey's Journey* to life in a way that words never could.

And, always, I must thank my husband for listening to my stories, encouraging me to be creative, and investing in the journey.

KELSEY LONIE

ONE CLEAR AND SUNNY DAY, the Fort Garry Horse Regiment marched in their first parade through the streets of Winnipeg, Manitoba.

Canada had just entered the Second World War, and these brave young men were training to become soldiers.

Hundreds of men, all dressed alike, marched in formation through the streets. They marched past smiling neighbours, a few stray cats, a boy on a bicycle,

two girls playing hopscotch, and a tiny collie puppy tied to the front porch of a large, well-kept house.

Even though the neighbours waved and the puppy barked, the men looked straight ahead, marching proudly in their new uniforms.

They were still marching when something caught the eye of one young soldier. “Don’t look now, but I think we have a new recruit,” he murmured to his friend, nodding behind him.

Sure enough, the little puppy had wiggled free from his leash and was marching alongside the men, wagging his tail and scampering to keep up.

The puppy followed the soldiers back to their barracks and curled up comfortably on a cot. But soon, an older man arrived, asking for his puppy.

Reluctantly, two young soldiers brought the little dog forward.

“He’s a determined fellow,” the taller, thinner soldier said. “He marched with us all the way back to our barracks.”

“Yes, he’d make a fine soldier,” the shorter soldier agreed. “What’s his name?”

“His name is Whitey,” said the older man as he hooked a leash firmly to the puppy’s collar. Whitey gave the soldiers a farewell lick, and they waved good-bye as he left the barracks with his owner.

The next day, as the men marched through town, Whitey saw them and barked excitedly! He wiggled and squirmed until he broke free from his leash and rejoined the men on parade.

“Well, what do you know!” the taller soldier remarked. “He really does want to join the army!”

Again, his owner arrived to pick up his puppy, and again, the soldiers reluctantly said good-bye to their new friend.

Day after day, the soldiers marched past Whitey's house, and each time the little dog broke free from his collar to join the army.

Eventually, the owner shrugged and said, "No matter how tightly I tie his leash, I can't seem to stop him from enlisting. He's all yours."

The soldiers cheered and welcomed Whitey into the Fort Garry Horse Regiment.

It did not take Whitey long to learn that there were many rules in the army.

Sometimes, it was okay to jump, run, and play tug-of-war with the soldiers.

Once, the men had a sports day, competing against other regiments. Whitey loved this! As the men competed in foot races, tug-of-war, and ball games, Whitey ran back and forth, barking and encouraging them.

Other times, it was important to stand very still while the soldiers were on inspection. When that happened, Whitey stood as tall as he could on his four little legs and remained as quiet as a mouse.

But, on the first word of command to “move off,” he would run to the front of the line to lead the way, proudly waving his tail like a flag.

Whitey's favourite part of army life was when the soldiers went on parade. Each morning, when the Sergeant Major shouted his orders to "fall in," Whitey would herd the men into their formations, barking at any slow movers to hurry up!

In all of his years with the Fort Garry Horse Regiment, Whitey never once missed a morning parade.

Whitey loved his men and was completely loyal to them. They all loved him in return. The soldiers took good care of their collie dog.

They clipped his nails.

They gave him baths.

They took him to the veterinarian for regular checkups.

They even brushed his teeth!

Eventually, he was given an official number, H260001/2, making him a true member of the Canadian Army.

"Trooper Whitey" was proud of his new status and even more proud to be given a soldier's pay of 35 cents a day, which he used to buy delicious treats!

Whitey followed the men of the Fort Garry Horse Regiment wherever they trained.

They even guarded prisoners at a camp in Ontario.

Whitey made it his personal responsibility to watch that no prisoners escaped.

Finally, the soldiers received orders to board a ship for England. The time had come to go to war.

As always, Whitey led the parade as the men marched towards the ship that would carry them across the ocean.

But just as they reached the gangplank, a red-faced man raised a hand and yelled, “Halt!”

Everyone froze in place, including Whitey, who stood as still as a statue, waiting for the man’s next command.

“Who owns this dog?” the red-faced man shouted.

The soldiers looked at each other, waiting for someone to speak up. Finally, a young man with freckles stepped forward.

“We all do, Sir. This is Trooper Whitey, and he is a soldier with the Canadian Army, Sir.”

The red-faced man's face grew redder, and he shook his head angrily.

"Dogs cannot board this ship. Dogs cannot join the army. Those are the rules."

No one dared to argue with this angry man, not even Whitey. He tucked his tail and lowered his ears, realizing that he had broken the rules.

A leash was clipped to Whitey's collar, and he was gently pulled away from his regiment by the freckled soldier.

"Come on, Whitey," the young man urged as Whitey resisted.

Whitey wanted to stay with his men!

When he realized that he was not allowed to board the ship, Whitey turned sadly and let the soldier lead him away.

However, rather than take Whitey back to the barracks, the freckled soldier led Whitey to a small office and placed him on a steel table.

"You've got to help us," the soldier begged a man in a white coat. "We've got to get Whitey onto that ship! He's a soldier, just like us!"

The medical officer looked at Whitey thoughtfully. "If I give him a sleeping pill, can you sneak him onto the ship?" he asked.

Whitey looked back and forth between the two men and gave a small wag of his tail to let them know that he was willing to give it a try.

The soldier with the freckles nodded eagerly, and the medical officer gave Whitey a pill. The pill tasted bad and made Whitey's eyes feel heavy.

As he drifted off to sleep, he felt himself being gently lifted into a warm, dark bed.

Little did he know that the bed was a cardboard box marked AMMUNITION! Two soldiers carried the box up the gangplank onto the ship where Whitey's men were waiting.

When Whitey woke up and saw the friendly faces of his fellow soldiers, he scampered around, licking any face in reach.

Onboard the ship, Whitey stayed hidden amongst the soldiers in their sleeping quarters as they sailed across the ocean. When they reached England, they smuggled him ashore.

The men continued to train overseas, marching on parade with Whitey always in the lead!

Sadly, like many other stories about war, this one does not have a happy ending. Trooper Whitey was one of many soldiers, civilians, and animals who gave their lives in the Second World War. He didn't make it home.

After serving his country as a military dog for almost five years, Whitey had a special military funeral with full honours and an eight-gun salute. He was lowered into a special grave near the south coast of England in May 1944, with a concrete tombstone to mark his spot.

Whitey was a Canadian soldier through and through. Even as a pup, Whitey wanted to be in the army, and no one could keep him away from the men of the Fort Garry Horse Regiment. He was loyal, kind, and loved by all who knew him. His fellow soldiers missed him deeply.

Whitey might be gone, but he has not been forgotten. Every time we think about Whitey, we remember that Canadian soldiers, some with two feet and others with four, gave their lives to protect us so that we can live in peace.

HISTORICAL NOTE

The Second World War broke out in September 1939 when Nazi Germany, led by Adolf Hitler, invaded Poland. Hitler was determined to take over as many countries as he could, eliminating all people who did not look and think like him, including Jewish people, people of colour, people with disabilities, Jehovah's Witnesses, Polish citizens, and members of the 2SLGBTQ+ community. On September 10, 1939, Canada joined the United Kingdom, France, and other Allied nations and declared war on Nazi Germany. More than one million Canadian men and women volunteered to fight the Nazis. It took many years, but eventually the Nazis and their supporters were defeated in 1945.

In 1939, a collie puppy named Whitey really did join the Canadian Army after tugging free from his leash to march with soldiers on parade in Winnipeg, Manitoba. In nearly five years with the Fort Garry Horse Regiment, Trooper Whitey never missed a morning parade. When the men were told to prepare for overseas duties and learned that dogs were not permitted on the ship, they bent the rules. Whitey was smuggled aboard the ocean liner SS *Oronsay* on the night of November 9, 1941, and sailed across the Atlantic Ocean with his men. He remained their mascot while in England, bringing joy and comfort to the regiment. Sadly, Whitey passed away while serving in England. He was given a full military funeral and eight-gun salute near the south coast of England in May 1944. One month later, the Fort

Garry Horse Regiment participated in D-Day, a battle that marked the beginning of the end of the Second World War.

Whitey was among thousands of dogs to serve in various roles during the Second World War. He was a regimental mascot—but other dogs were trained to carry messages or telephone wire across great distances, detect danger before their handlers, pull supplies through deep snow, and find injured soldiers in need of help. They served bravely and calmly in the face of danger, using their highly developed senses to save many lives. Today, dogs continue to perform a variety of highly skilled jobs in the military. Many dogs and soldiers returned to Canada after the Second World War with battle scars, sad memories, and a sense of pride in standing up for what was right. But not everyone came home. The privileges Canadians enjoy today are largely due to the brave soldiers, some with two legs and others with four, who put themselves in harm's way to keep us safe. Next time you stand at a Remembrance Day ceremony, wear a poppy, or see a Canadian in uniform, say a little thank you to the brave men and women who protect your freedoms. And don't forget to thank the brave dogs like Whitey who serve our country too.

RACHEL BUHR, STILL LIFE PHOTOGRAPHY

KELSEY LONIE was raised on a cattle ranch in Southern Saskatchewan, a setting that shaped her passion for both history and animals. She grew up cherishing her grandparents' stories about life during the Second World War and has dedicated her career to making this story accessible, engaging, and relevant. Kelsey holds a BEd and an MA in History from the University of Regina and specializes in the contributions of western Canadians at home and overseas during the Second World War. She and her husband live in Regina, Saskatchewan, with their dog and cat.

TANNER HANSEN

RENEE HANSEN is an illustrator, born and raised on the prairies of Southern Saskatchewan. Her childhood was filled with artistic influences and imagination, which encouraged her love of creating. Telling stories has been the goal of her artwork since she was very young. Renee lives near Bromhead, Saskatchwan, with her husband and son.